W9-CNA-979

COMMUNITY HELPERS

Librarians

by Kate Moening

BELLWETHER MEDIA • MINNEAPOLIS, MN

Note to Librarians, Teachers, and Parents:

Blastoff! Readers are carefully developed by literacy experts and combine standards-based content with developmentally appropriate text.

Level 1 provides the most support through repetition of high-frequency words, light text, predictable sentence patterns, and strong visual support.

Level 2 offers early readers a bit more challenge through varied simple sentences, increased text load, and less repetition of high-frequency words.

Level 3 advances early-fluent readers toward fluency through increased text and concept load, less reliance on visuals, longer sentences, and more literary language.

Level 4 builds reading stamina by providing more text per page, increased use of punctuation, greater variation in sentence patterns, and increasingly challenging vocabulary.

Level 5 encourages children to move from "learning to read" to "reading to learn" by providing even more text, varied writing styles, and less familiar topics.

Whichever book is right for your reader, Blastoff! Readers are the perfect books to build confidence and encourage a love of reading that will last a lifetime!

This edition first published in 2019 by Bellwether Media, Inc.

No part of this publication may be reproduced in whole or in part without written permission of the publisher. For information regarding permission, write to Bellwether Media, Inc., Attention: Permissions Department, 6012 Blue Circle Drive, Minnetonka, MN 55343.

Library of Congress Cataloging-in-Publication Data

LC record for Librarians available at https://lccn.loc.gov/2017057756

Editor: Christina Leaf   Designer: Brittany McIntosh

Printed in the United States of America, North Mankato, MN.

Table of Contents

Book Search

Jason needs a **library** book for his homework. He asks the librarian for help.

The librarian shows Jason how to find his book. Now he can find books by himself!

What Are Librarians?

Librarians help people find **information** and do **research**.

Many librarians
work in schools.
Others are in
public libraries.

What Do Librarians Do?

Librarians buy books for their libraries. They help people borrow these books to take home.

Librarians help with research. They guide people to the right books or **web sites**.

Librarian Gear

computer   books   book cart   book scanner

15

Librarians host **community events**, too. They read books aloud for story time!

What Makes a Good Librarian?

Librarians know a lot. They can **communicate** this knowledge to many different people.

Librarian Skills

✓ good communicators   ✓ organized

✓ good at research   ✓ problem-solvers

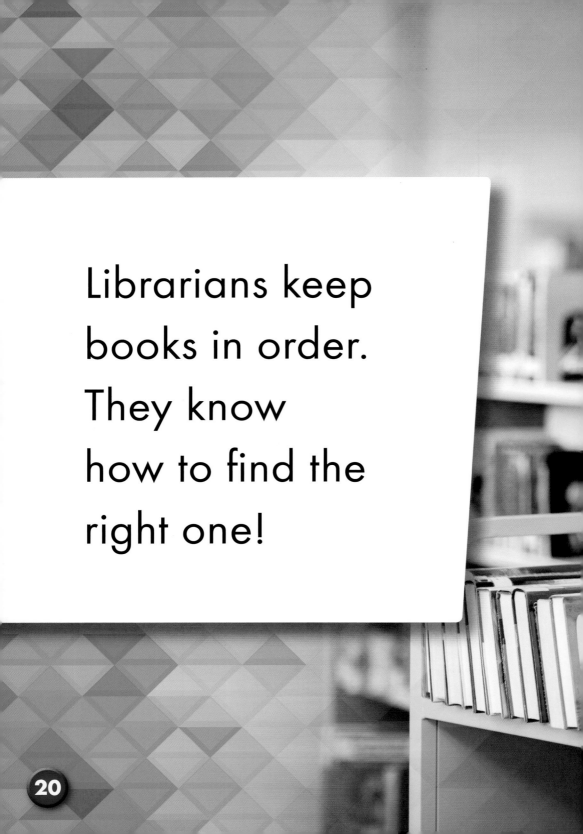

Librarians keep
books in order.
They know
how to find the
right one!

Glossary

communicate

to share information

library

a place where people use or borrow books and other materials

community events

times when people gather to do an activity together

research

to look for information or study

information

facts and knowledge

web sites

Internet pages run by a person or organization